WHERE AM I?

WHAT'S MY CURRENT SITUATION?

Stand STRONG

Part Two: Will Learns to Ask Powerful Questions

Cool stuff for college (and life)!

A College Survival Guidebook With Practices For Your Success

Luckett Davidson

WHAT DO I WANT?

HOW WILL I GET THERE?

Printed and bound in the United States of America
ISBN: 978-1-7333434-1-1

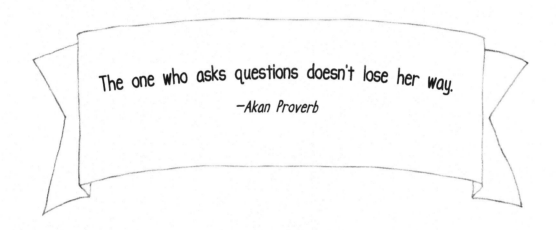

The one who asks questions doesn't lose her way.

—Akan Proverb

WILL

Stand STRONG, Part Two

Will's Story and *Powerful Questions*

CONTENTS

WEATHER NERD

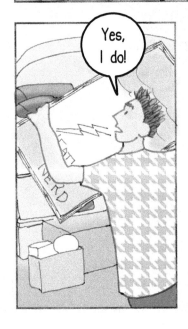

4

POWERFUL QUESTIONS

WHAT

HOW

WHERE

WHEN

WHO

- 🌀 **OPEN-ENDED**
  Cannot be answered by YES or NO

- 🌀 Related to **VALUES**

- 🌀 **CREATIVITY** building

- 🌀 Drive **LEARNING** and **ACTION**

- 🌀 Avoid **WHY**

FIRST THESE	FOLLOW with THESE
• Where are you? • What is the current situation?	• What is good about it? • What is not good? • What is most important about it?
• What do you want? • What is the desired outcome?	• What do you envision in six months? • What supports will show up? What barriers? • How do your actions align with what you say you want?
• How are you going to get there? • When will you get started?	• What resources do you need? • Who will help hold you accountable?

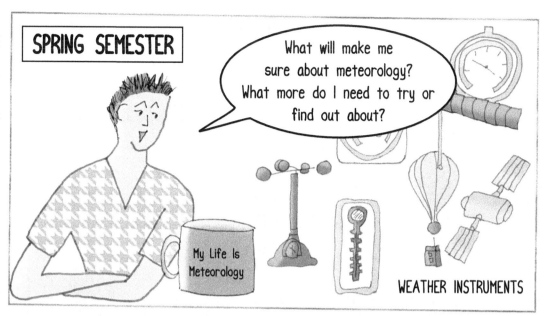

SPRING SEMESTER

What will make me sure about meteorology? What more do I need to try or find out about?

My Life Is Meteorology

WEATHER INSTRUMENTS

CAREERS

SOCIOLOGY

POLITICAL SCIENCE

METEOROLOGY CLUB

Got my grades today. Wonder what Dad will say.

FOXSTONE UNIVERSITY
Student Academic Report – SPRING Semester

William Lloyd IV	170	Problem Solving & Programming	3	B	3	9
	132	American History	3	C	2	6
	152	Political Science	3	C	2	6
Grade Point	142	Sociology	3	C	2	6
Average	122	Meteorology	3	A	4	12
2.4			15	Sem Credit		39
				Hrs Extended		

Thanks for showing me your grades, Will. What are you thinking now?

Another A in meteorology made me believe I can do the work I'm passionate about. Thank you for your help with this.

WEATHE NERD

POWERFUL QUESTIONS helped me think about what's going on in my life.

Now I can use them to figure out how to talk to Dad and Mom about my new plans.

20

What are some of the challenges Will faced in his first year of college?
What do you think he learned?
Write and draw and share.

EXPLORE YOUR OWN STORY

with

POWERFUL QUESTIONS

_____

(YOUR NAME)

Learns to Ask Powerful Questions

_____

(DATE)

Stand STRONG, Part Two

Here's your chance to use what you saw in my story to figure out something in your own life.

You'll work on it in the following pages.

WHAT YOU'LL NEED:

* This book
* Willingness to think about your own story
* Pen or pencil
* Colored pencils or markers

WHAT YOU'LL DO:

* Make notes and/or images about something in your life (Use any large or small issue that's on your mind right now)
* Center yourself. You learned how from Coleman's story, Part One of Stand STRONG
* Use POWERFUL QUESTIONS to consider
    Where are you?
    What do you want?
    How are you going to get there?
* Plan steps to take action toward What You Want.
* Decide on some small steps you'll take right away to move toward your goal
* Share your thoughts and plans with someone like a classmate or mentor

WHAT?
HOW?
WHERE?
WHO?
WHEN?

You can start your POWERFUL QUESTION session by practicing Stand STRONG (like Coleman did) for a few breaths.

This is how I look when I Stand STRONG.

Stand STRONG practice

Stand in your usual way
Exaggerate it a little
THEN
<u>Plant</u> your feet hip-width apart
Balance your weight front to back
Line up your spine from the base to the top of your head as if suspended by a string from above
Level your chin
Line up your ears with your shoulders
Breathe in, then exhale
NOW say
I CAN DO IT!

FROM SLOUCH to STAND STRONG

Remember how Coleman moved from a slouch to Standing STRONG?

When you think about your own life, what's an area that you want to improve or a decision that you are struggling with? This can be something big or something small. Write and draw a simple statement about it.

Ben showed me how to use Powerful Questions on my big decision about what I want to study. Since then, I've asked myself Powerful Questions to make lots of other decisions. They've helped me understand my situation, what I want and how to get there.

Decisions like:
* How to manage study and climate research time
* When to save and when to spend
* Whether to get a sociology tutor
* Should I move off campus next year?

Using the statement you wrote on Page 25, ask yourself 3 or 4 Powerful Questions about it. On this page concentrate on what's good or going well. Write, draw and share your questions and your answers.

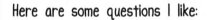

Here are some questions I like:

* What's good about where I am right now?
* What is most important to me right now?
* What do I love to practice?
* How could I work less and achieve more?
* What could I release to make space for something new?
* What am I most passionate about?
* Where do I find joy and energy?

Sticking with that same statement (from page 25),
ask yourself some Powerful Questions about what's NOT going so well.
Write and draw and share your answers.

Here are some questions to help you:

* What do I want to change?
* Where am I stuck?
* What actions are keeping me stuck?
* How will I feel if nothing changes?
* What thoughts are keeping me from changing?
* What are the barriers to moving forward on this?
* What makes this difficult for me?
* What else is affected by where I am now?

Now that you've thought "where AM I?" you have information that will help you consider "what DO I want?" Ask yourself several POWERFUL QUESTIONS. Write, draw and share.

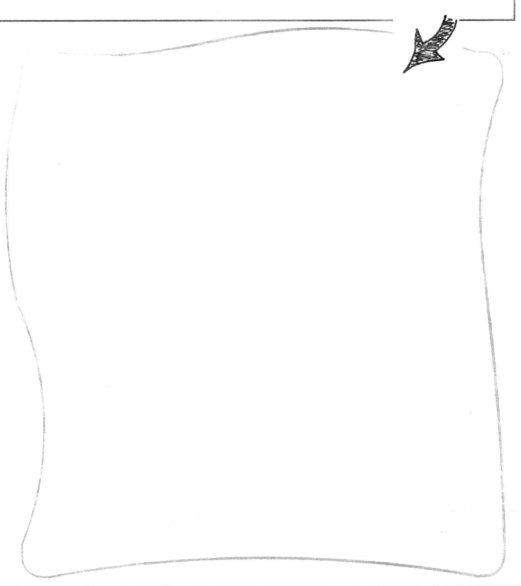

Some questions I've found useful:

* If I didn't want to please anyone else, what would I want?
* If I keep doing what I'm doing now,
  where will I be in six months?
* Where would I like to be?
* What gives me joy and energy?
* What makes me anxious and worried?

Write a simple statement of your goal or commitment (based on the questions you've asked and answered on the previous pages). Draw an image that represents your commitment. Then share.

In my story, this is my commitment:

I will get ready to talk to my folks about studying meteorology instead of prelaw.

Think about what you want based on your commitment
from the last page, then ask yourself "HOW AM I GOING TO GET THERE?"
Write and draw and share.

These questions work for me:

* What am I doing now that will help me get what I want?
* What do I want to change or do differently?
* What solutions open for me if I stop worrying
  and think more deeply and creatively?
* What am I curious about that the
  questions brought up?
* Who could help me think about solutions?

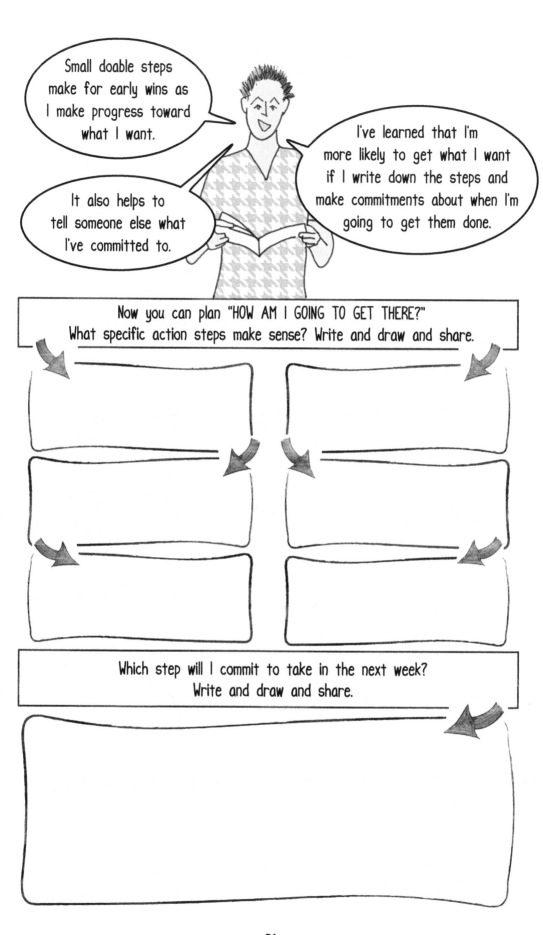

YOU'RE ON YOUR WAY!

You've just completed Part Two of Stand STRONG, a series that will help you navigate new experiences and stay calm in the midst of major changes.

You can use the tools, practices and concepts to survive college and create the life you want in college and beyond.

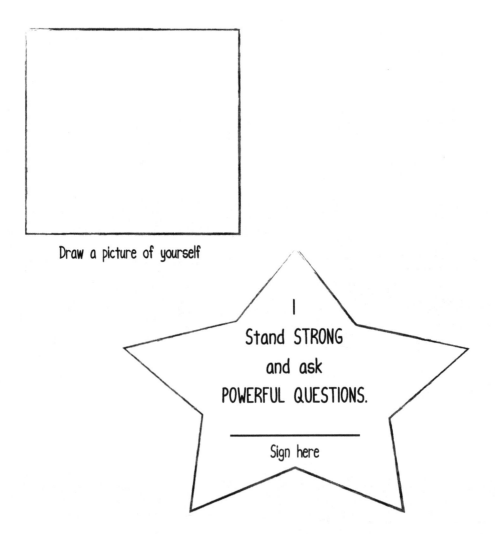

Draw a picture of yourself

I
Stand STRONG
and ask
POWERFUL QUESTIONS.

_____
Sign here

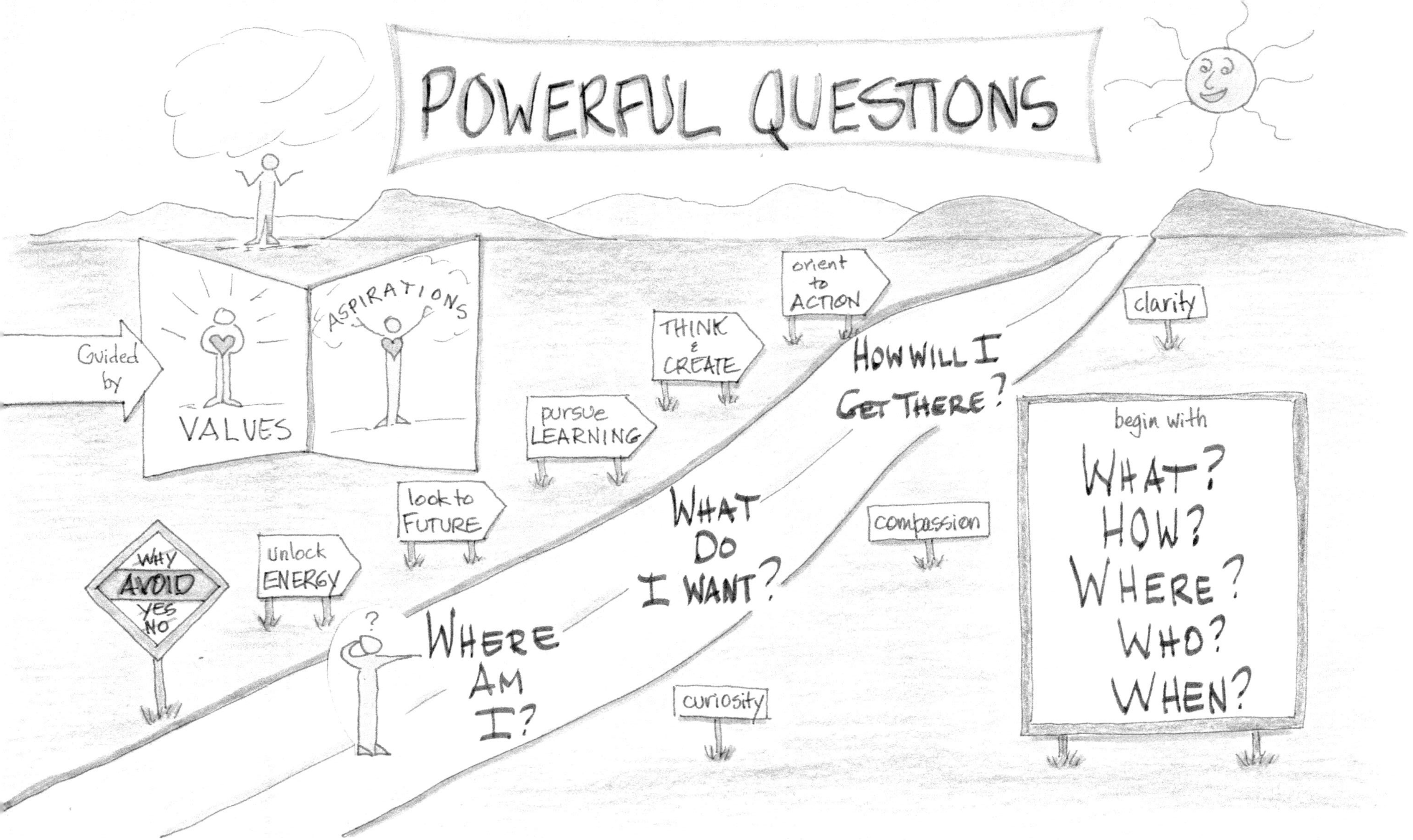
POWERFUL QUESTIONS
Guided by
VALUES
ASPIRATIONS
WHY
AVOID
YES
NO
unlock ENERGY
look to FUTURE
pursue LEARNING
THINK & CREATE
orient to ACTION
clarity
WHERE AM I?
WHAT DO I WANT?
HOW WILL I GET THERE?
curiosity
compassion
begin with
WHAT?
HOW?
WHERE?
WHO?
WHEN?

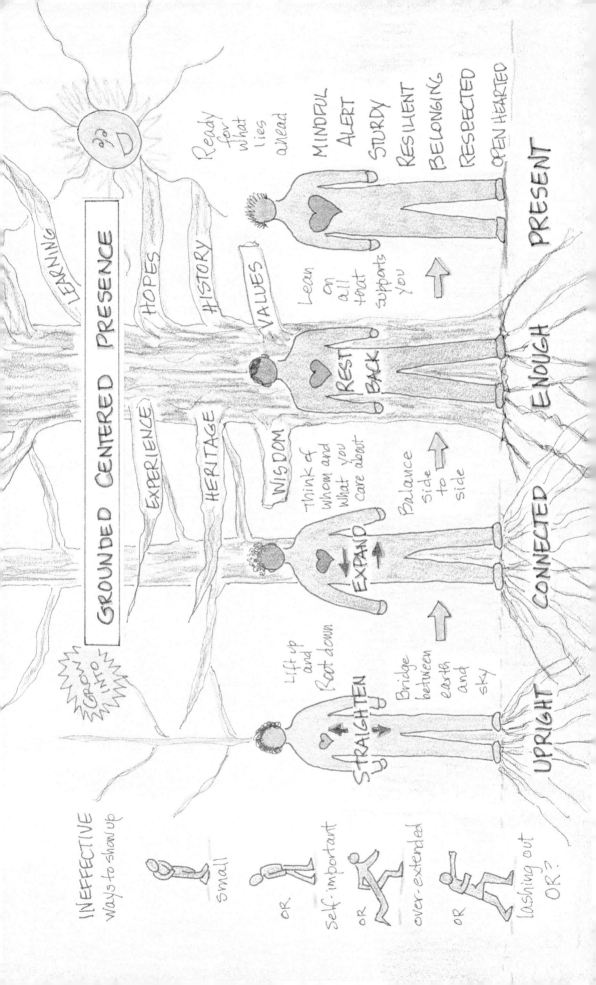

GROUNDED CENTERED PRESENCE

GROW INTO

LEARNING

HOPES
HISTORY
EXPERIENCE
HERITAGE

VALUES
Lean on all that supports you

Ready for what lies ahead

MINDFUL
ALERT
STURDY
RESILIENT
BELONGING
RESPECTED
OPEN HEARTED

PRESENT

WISDOM
Think of whom and what you care about

REST BACK

EXPAND
Balance side to side

ENOUGH

STRAIGHTEN
Lift up and Root down

Bridge between earth and sky

CONNECTED

UPRIGHT

INEFFECTIVE
Ways to show up

small

OR.

self important

OR.

over-extended

OR

lashing out
OR?

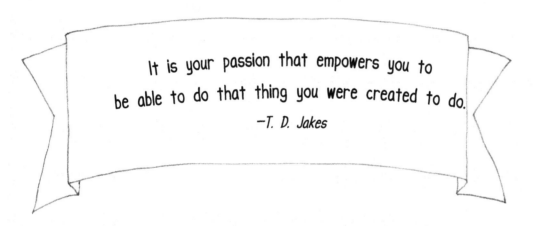

It is your passion that empowers you to
be able to do that thing you were created to do.
—T. D. Jakes

GRATITUDE

Kentucky Foundation for Women
Network Center for Community Change
Doug Silsbee & Bebe Hansen, Presence-Based Coaching®
Jill Adams and Change Makers, Jefferson Community and Technical College
Christy Metzger, First Year Experience, University of Louisville
Alexandra Thrustone, St. Francis School
Janelle Rae, Spalding University
Amy Hirschy, University of Louisville
Lisa Millsaps, Western High School
Tofte Lake Center and Liz Engleman
Jean Johnson and Barbara Hulburt
Lyedie Geer, Practicing Artists Lab
Grace Christiansen and David Temin
Guy Davidson and John Catlett
Elizabeth Neyman and Alex Haynes
Frank Steele, Editor
Karen Abney
Amari and Althea Dryden
Bethany Kelly, Publishing Partner
Stefan Merour, Graphic designer

Danica Novgorodoff, graphic novelist
Keith Look
Mikki and David Little
Amanda Blake, Embright
Shelton McElroy
Cassandra Webb
Mimi Zinniel
Liza Little
Jan Calvert
Ebony O'Rea
Nola and McGee Catlett
Jennie Jean Davidson
Steve Woodring
Witters
Rowing Sisters
Sarah Halley
Carey Goldstein
Jessica Bellamy
Pam Greenwell
Julie Wunderlin
Last Thursday Book Club

CITATIONS

Powerful Questions:
The Wunderlin Company
Presence-Based Coaching®
Leadership that Works
Network Center for Community Change

Luckett Davidson, a leadership development coach, writer and illustrator, lives with her family in Louisville, Kentucky.

Luckett's take on the personal skills required for college survival is grounded in her studies and explorations in Presence-Based Coaching®, community organizing, the food industry, and fine arts as well as lived experience.

Touchstone Guides presents **Stand STRONG**, a series that supports students through the transition from high school to college. This unique, interactive series allows students to personalize their growth by reflecting and practicing new skills and habits of self-awareness and leadership presence.

In **Part One,** Coleman learns to Center and watches his confidence soar.

In **Part Two,** Will learns to ask Powerful Questions as he considers big and small decisions.

In **Part Three,** Shayla learns how the Accountability Pathway can help her make progress toward major goals.

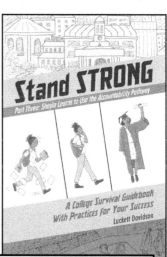

Join them as they journey through the challenges of college and learn to build inner strength, seek support and stand strong!

Visit our website www.touchstoneguides.com to download the Stand Strong Tips for Session Leaders. These handy tips support those wishing to lead a small group! Posters are also available on the website for purchase.

Bulk and nonprofit rates are available. Contact us for more information at luckett@touchstoneguides.com.

Touchstone Guides explore the intersection of coaching skills, practices and accessible and memorable images. Compassion, resonance, grace and resilience are the touchstones of our work.

CPSIA information can be obtained
at www.ICGtesting.com
Printed in the USA
JSHW062358300523
42404JS00004B/248

9 781733 343411